MAKE IT YOUR BITCH

THE ULTIMATE GUIDE
TO OWNING LIFE

UNEARTHING YOUR
PASSiON &
purpose
TO FIND EXPLOSIVE
HAPPINESS

By Tracy Porter
th John Porter and A. Wilding Wells
Copyright 2016 Tracy Porter
All designs, graphics and artwork
By Tracy Porter ©2016

D0955087

WWW.MAKEITYOURBITCH.NET
WWW.POETICWANDERLUST.COM
WWW.AWILDINGWELLS.COM

HYP NOTIC PRESS

VERBA POETICA

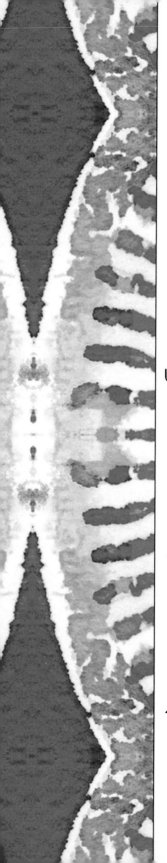
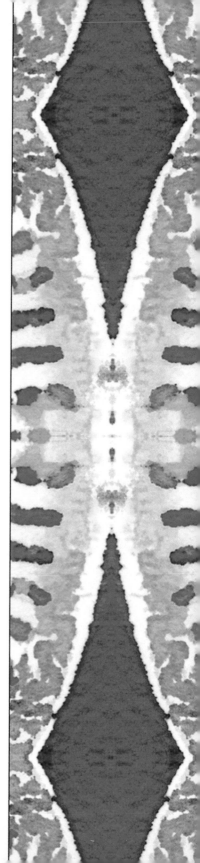

Dear lovely
reader~

This book is
for you
because
you're
already
believing in
yourself by
wanting to
unearth your
passion and
purpose!

For you,
because
you've
decided you
want to live
your days
filled with...

explosive
happiness
xxx,
TP'

It's oh-dark-thirty. I'm flat on my back, eyes pinned to the nothingness above my bed. I pat the side table for my pen and paper, only to find they're missing. Fuck! Ideas storm my brain, endless details and images clogging the pipes. I huff out a long sign and squirm around while knuckling my forehead. It's way too early to get up, and too dark and cold. Thorough reasoning completed, I still lay wide awake.

My husband sputters out something sandwiched between a snore and a mumble, "No, Syd, our car's where I left it". WTF? Who the fuck is "Syd"? And what's he doing with our fucking car?

More ideas rain down from the darkness. It's okay, I can sleep when I'm dead.

Butterflies zip through my belly at hurricane speeds at the thought of my day. I'm so excited: I'm starting another novel. I can't get to it fast enough!

Do you feel like that most mornings? Out of your gourd, crazy excited to start your day?

WHAT IS TRUE FOR YOU? IS EXPLOSIVE HAPPINESS YOUR TRUTH? OR ARE BULLSHIT LIMITATIONS CLOUDING YOUR PERCEPTION, YOUR PATH TO ENLIGHTENMENT AND YOUR ABILITY TO SECURE EXPLOSIVE HAPPINESS?

LUCK WON'T BRING YOU EXPLOSIVE HAPPINESS, UNLESS YOU'VE HARNESSED YOUR INNER MAGICAL SUPER POWERS. AND, IF THAT'S THE CASE, WHY AREN'T YOU TIME-TRAVELLING, READING TERRORISTS' MINDS FOR THE FBI AND SOLVING WORLD HUNGER? FLYING AROUND WOULD BE SUPER COOL, WOULDN'T IT?

THE TRUTH IS, YOU *CAN* GET YOURSELF TO THE TASTY LAND OF EXPLOSIVE HAPPINESS. IT IS ABSOLUTELY POSSIBLE. I'M NOT SAYING IT'LL BE EASY. BUT I AM SAYING THERE'S A PATH AND ONLY YOU REALLY KNOW THE WAY. I CAN HELP - THIS BOOK WILL HELP - BUT IN THE END IT'S COMPLETELY UP TO YOU.

BUST YOUR ASS, WHILE CONQUERING YOUR FEARS, EXPLORING YOUR CREATIVITY AND ADVANCING YOUR SKILLS AS YOU NAVIGATE THE UNKNOWN AND POWER THROUGH OBSTACLES. OH, AND... FAIL AND FAIL AND FAIL. NOT TOO SEXY.

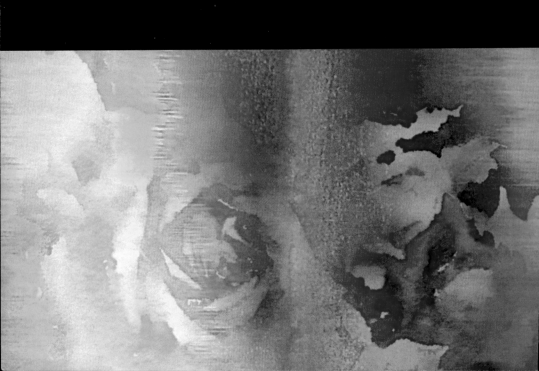

Me? I'm a serial entrepreneur and up-failer. I'm also the ringmaster of a Noah's Arc-full of animals that are my muses, and the mom of four boys. I'm not Harvard-educated. Nor am I a doctor, a billionaire or a self-help guru. I am me, a closet full of shortcomings and hard-earned successes with a big helping of whoopass who lives explosively happy days.

I wasn't born in the projects or raised by wolves on a remote island — I was blessed to have kind, nurturing, non-coddling, no bullshit parents. I am though a girl who earned her degree from the school of hard knocks — otherwise known as failing up — while unearthing my passion and purpose. Through it all I've taught myself the steps to be, on most days, explosively happy. "Most" isn't "Perfect", but "Perfect" doesn't exist. "Most" is pretty fucking awesome.

"MOST" IS PRETTY FUCKING AWESOME.

The purpose of this book is – and my hope is – that this book drills into your soul and inspires you to think of all kinds of scrumptious, mind-blowing things. But *NOT to* overthink. That would be ugly bad, LA-traffic bad.

Overthinking kills. It's chloroform to the soul and the brain. Overthinking ought to be banned, considering the number of great ideas its killed. It might be more toxic than clostridium botulinum. Uh, don't overthink that. Just trust me, it's badass deadly.

Passion, on the other hand, is a riddle wrapped in a mystery, inside an enigma. How's that for unattainable. It's been promised as the holy grail of happiness.

But is it?

CAPRICIOUS BUSYNESS
IS NOT PROGRESS.

EVERYONE IS BUSY.
WHO'S GETTING SHIT
DONE? VERY FEW.

achieve happiness on that principle alone? Your skeptic antennae ought to be vibrating right about now.

"Follow your passion!" This and dozens of similar sounding copycat quotes have been wallpapered in our minds all our lives by everyone from the fat cats of Madison Avenue to the coifed, buffed and plumped nightly news anchors. Bittersweet as it is, I feel they're sort of selling a fairy tale. No, worse than that, it's pretty much bullshit.

What we weren't told about passion is it comes with strings – big fat hairy slick and slimy strings…and here you thought this was going to be a fluff book because of the pretty cover.

We were encouraged to believe the simple act of *following our passion* would lead us to happiness, riches and self-fulfillment. It makes sense based on all the other lies we grew up believing. A tooth under your pillow brings you wealth! Only good girls and boys are on Santa's gift list. Good grades land you the dream job… Yeah, right.

IT'S OKAY TO
WONDER IF WHAT
YOU'RE DOING IS
GOOD ENOUGH.

"FOLLOW YOUR PASSION!"

It's a pretty misleading statement. That said, I bought into the argument early on. Heck, I may as well have been the poster child for it.

The hitch for many is they think identifying their passion is the objective, and that everything else in life will fall into place. Understandably so, it's the unexplained secret. And truthfully, most people want effortless; they want to forget there are realities and routes and obstacles and zombies with hatchets who want to hack into your dreamy idea of passion.

I've come to loathe the word "passion" so much, I almost didn't use it in this book. But I decided to stick with the perceived sexy word and give her a nice little makeover.

I am passionate, yes, *but...* *("yes, but", that's funny - say that five times fast).* I am also obsessively disciplined and purposeful in how I approach my days. This is because I'm terrified that I might not get to spend my time autonomously, doing what I want to do - making a living creating while feeling happy-as-all-get-out.

I can't offer perfect solutions to everyone's situations. Nor will I propose pseudoscience drivel that reeks of pixie dust. At times in my life though I was sure that sort of thinking would get me everything I ever wanted.

Maybe I wasn't trying hard enough for the universe to embrace *my* wishes? I tried believing it was possible. *Think it with every cell in your body and it will happen.* Apparently my internal and external vibrations weren't aligned and synchronizing with every cell in my body to emotionalize the harmony with my polarity.

What the fuck does that mean? Good question.

What about accountability and reflection? What about taking responsibility for needing and wanting explosive happiness, versus assuming the vast universe would take care of me if I manifested my conscious and subconscious like other "super humans."

I don't subscribe to cult-speak or manipulative marketing that implies merely wishing for something will get you everything you want. It's a wee bit too cosmic for me, though apparently 1% of all people who embrace this presumption claim it miraculously works – 1%!? Now that's conversion!

YOU CAN FIND
PASSION,
PURPOSE AND
HAPPINESS
WHEN YOU
HAVE THE
MINDSET YOU
ARE WILLING
TO PUSH
THROUGH
STUMBLING
BLOCKS. THIS
TAKES GUTS
AND
INTEGRITY
AND
DOGGEDNESS.

I believe the idea that optimism along with a good dose of realism is a more versatile path to happiness.

And the truth is, thoughts without action often equals disappointment. That's just plain scientific... just as you can plainly see in this example where "T" is your collective thoughts and "L" is your loser cousin, Lenny, and "a" is your asshole boss:

$$T/\mu + f(x)^\circ = a_0 + \sum_{n=1}^{\infty} \left(a_n \frac{n\pi x}{L} + b_n{}^3{}_a\sin\frac{n\pi x}{L} \right)$$

Too bad the laws of attraction are

Waiting around and trusting
everything will magically fall into
place in its own good time is *one*
method, much like the idea that
staring at the phone will make it
ring...
Why not try it? What do you have to
lose? I won't point out the obvious
elephant in the room.
Okay, I lied. I can't help myself in
regards to that sweet little
elephant, because doing nothing –
aka waiting around hoping but
taking no steps toward what you
want – could be the end of your
career and/or happiness. And that
would be a damn shame.
I don't lack compassion and I am not
a heartless ogre. I'm rough-and-
ready down-to-earth. I've been an
entrepreneur since I was twenty –
that's over twenty-five years. I'm
jaded, a grizzled veteran, a G.I. Jane
with life-like appendages.

DON'T FUCK WITH ME!

I'VE EARNED MY FEET-ON-
THE-GROUND BADGE.

YES, THERE IS GREATNESS
OUT THERE; I FEEL IT
MASSIVELY.

I BELIEVE IN THE AWE
AND WONDER OF THE
UNIVERSE.

THERE IS ALSO GREATNESS
INSIDE YOU - IN EACH OF
US - THAT IS ACHING TO
BE HARNESSED NOW.

NOT TOMORROW.

NOT NEXT WEEK.

TO-FUCKING-DAY!

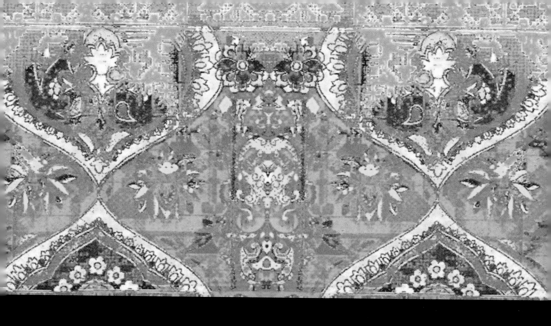

There is no entry fee or gold rope or degree needed to take a leap of faith in yourself.

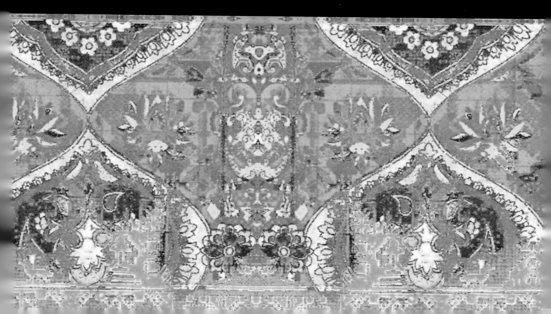

So – here it is (and what I mean by "it" is a really long run-on sentence... ready?) – I believe one potential path toward achieving happiness has a lot to do with creating and sticking to routine and embracing and building on incremental shifts in your everyday, small steps and pivots, together with strengthening your skills and evaluating *truthfully* how you're doing in your day-to-day, a balanced path; recognizing that creativity is one of your greatest assets, no matter what your career is or what phase in life you are in, is another.

Dude, that sentence was longer than a summer sunset in Finland.

Saying you are not creative is like saying you're incapable of thinking. You must (and there should be a law) change the conversation in your head if you think you're not creative.

I am a strong believer that once you're really good at something – because of colossal effort and smarts to focus on this thing – creativity explodes right alongside happiness.

Sounds awesome doesn't it? It definitely is.

Will it be easy? Nope. It's work.

But we have to work anyway so why not zero in on getting great at something you like and creating a routine that moves it forward. Why wouldn't someone want this? Fear of being ridiculed or judged? What's the worst thing that could happen? Oh, yeah...judgment and ridicule....

Bitch, please!

THIS BOOK IS FILLED WITH
HEAPS OF DOWN AND DIRTY
SCRUMPTIOUS TIDBITS OF
MOTIVATION, INSPIRATION,
TIPS AND TECHNIQUES,
SANDWICHED BETWEEN DEAD-ON
GET-YOUR-ASS-MOVING
GUIDANCE.

I DON'T BELIEVE ANYONE WANTS
RAH-RAH PROMISES AS
GUIDANCE. REAL PROBLEMS NEED
REAL SOLUTIONS. THIS HOW-TO
GUIDE OF GRIT-FILLED
GOODNESS AND ACTION-PROMPTS
WILL BE ESPECIALLY USEFUL
WHEN YOU NEED A SHOVE FROM
SOMEONE WHO'S BEEN WHERE YOU
ARE. WHICH IS - I ASSUME -
IN NEED OF THE
AFOREMENTIONED SANDWICH.

I LIKE TO THINK IT'S LOW ON
BULLSHIT AND HIGH ON GET-
THE-FUCK-GOING. IT IS NOT A
CINDERELLA BOOK. MY YEARS IN
THE TRENCHES HAVE BEEN
ANYTHING BUT CINDERELLA.
EXCEPT FOR THE RISING-FROM-
THE-ASHES PART

But the reality is, job dissatisfaction, anxiety and uncertainty are at all-time highs in our culture. Some things can be difficult to cope with if you don't have continuous reminders. If you don't use your I-got-this muscle every day, navigating can be, at best, tricky.

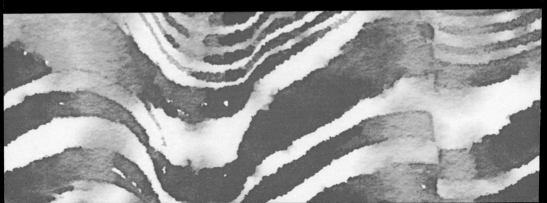

Success is measured differently by everyone. To me, it means being the gatekeeper of my life. I'm a work in progress, constantly tweaking, hacking and evaluating the way I function.

I work hard to keep fear of failure out of my emotion bank, even though I fail plenty. Failing is horrid, but it's an indispensable way to learn if you are able to dissect the 'why' and 'how' of it. Not easy but doable, and essential.

Regardless of your fears, vulnerabilities, lack of direction, age, financial situation, marital status and/or college degree(s) - or lack thereof - I'm certain the tidbits in this book will inspire you to unearth your passion, happiness and purpose.

WHY TRUST ME? DON'T. IF YOU WANT PERFECT.

Feeling passionate about your day-to-day is healing, exciting and mind expanding. But harnessing passion and backing it with a stockpile of kick-ass tools AND a plan is *way* more fulfilling. My aim is that you can use this guide as a manifesto to get inspired, feel encouraged and - most important - take action. Also, consider it a reminder that you have the potential to live your passion and purpose every single day with these principles.

Academically, I was a 'C' student. I failed more than one class in high school. Written tests and memorization skills were my greatest downfalls. I was a creative. It's where I thrived. And, sadly, that's still at the bottom of the list when it comes to our current academic environment.

To be clear, I'm pro-Math, Science and English. But everything should be couched in creativity. EVERYTHING!

Scared stiff of failure, I skipped over the entire math section on my SAT's, and was told afterwards by one of my favorite teachers that I would never be successful in life. *("in life"?? 'cuz I skipped a section of the SAT's.)*

Luckily, my parents told me "success" came in all sizes, shapes and colors. Just like people. My parents were – and still are – the absolute bomb.

IF WE PRANCE AROUND IN NON-
STOP PRAISE-OURSELVES MODE...
HOW CAN WE EXPECT TO GROW?

Thankfully, I loved making all kinds of things and my parents encouraged it, as they saw it bring me confidence where my grades often crushed me to my core.

Four days after graduation from high school I was gone. I won a modeling contest in New York and a ticket to Paris to boot. I crossed the pond to explore whatever Europe had to offer and give modeling a shot.

I had no idea at the time that I was entering entrepreneur boot camp. Modeling is not entrepreneurship but I was on an accelerated course of sales, marketing, constant re-invention and learning how to package me. I was humbled and then some, time and again. "No" was my constant reminder that I was not special. I was continually told I was not exceptional in any way.

I was told that I needed a nose job, a boob job, have my ears pinned back, grow two inches, create a waist, wear hazel contact lenses and be someone – or something – I wasn't.

Demoralization wasn't just a code word, it was how I lived for almost two years. Thanks to my strong spine, I said no to all of their requests to change me, the best product I had. All the while, I continued to make things – craft things or develop products – on the side.

I'd sew clothes, decorate shoes with vintage junk jewels, paint silk scarves and craft jewelry. I'd troll scrap yards for supplies, then turn odd old bits into funky home furnishings. This was my passion; this was my calling. It made me happy. But could it be my purpose? Could I have a career making things?

TAKE THE NEXT BITE.

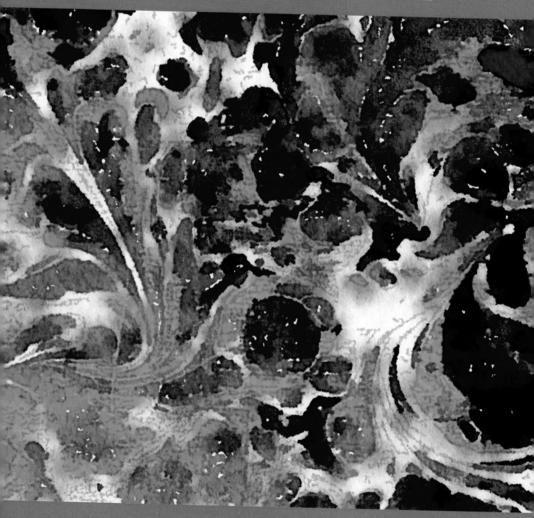

PROGRESS IS CRUCIAL.

Most people told me to narrow my focus and take some classes, maybe get a degree to solve my dilemma. I was often advised to consider the practical applications of art, such as architecture or graphic design. Something that could lead to a *real* job. *(dancing in my head all during that time was 'fuck that; I got this. I just need to focus and move forward')*

I had always thought art school would be an incredible journey to explore, though I always assumed I would never be able to get in based on my crappy high school grades.

I was mostly right. Even art schools wanted kids who tested well on their SAT's. But, after much conversation, negotiating, and working my tail off on a portfolio to make a good impression on the admissions folks, The Art Institute of Chicago *permitted* me to hand over a mammoth wad of cash and enroll in a few classes.

Man, was I stoked!

I pulled ten thousand dollars out of my hard-earned savings account and handed it over to these folks with more belief in the system than I should have had. I thought and assumed I was investing in me. But only a few months in it didn't feel like it was about my education so much as it was about their system.

I was certain college was going to kill my creativity and spirit. I was chomping at the bit for more, and too hungry to stay. So after trying out a few classes, and feeling nothing but duped, I walked away. One of my professors offered to buy my class project; I gave it to her.

A month later, at the age of twenty, realizing limits are bullshit and that I had nothing to lose, I started my first business. Though it was short-lived, I learned a good deal about my truths, and grit, plus a little about what it takes to make your passion purposeful. But the most important thing I learned was a shit-ton about explosive happiness, and how I wasn't going to live any other way.

AT TWENTY-THREE, I MARRIED MY
FAVORITE PERSON. TWENTY-FIVE
YEARS LATER I STILL KNOW IT
WAS THE RIGHT CHOICE.
TOGETHER WE'VE STARTED EIGHT
COMPANIES. FAMILY, FRIENDS,
EMPLOYEES AND INVESTORS ALL
HELPING THINGS PROGRESS AS WE
GREW.

WE HAVE DESIGNED EVERYTHING
FROM APPAREL, SHOES AND
JEWELRY TO TABLEWARE, FABRIC,
SINKS, FURNITURE, RUGS,
LIGHTING, WALL ART AND MORE.
HOW? BECAUSE WE BELIEVED WE
COULD. THEN WE TOOK MICRO-
STEPS TO MAKE THINGS HAPPEN.
WE DIDN'T JUST DREAM. WE DID.
THERE IS A BIG FAT HAIRY
DIFFERENCE.

WE'VE WRITTEN ALMOST TWENTY
BOOKS. ON TOPICS RANGING FROM
HOME DECORATING TO
ENTERTAINING TO SEXY EROTIC
ROMANCE NOVELS.

Words
	and
		images
			are
				free.

We have sold our designs to the largest retailers in the world: Target, Costco, Bed Bath and Beyond, Macy's, Bloomingdales, Nordstrom, Neiman Marcus, QVC, HSN and so forth. And in the process, we've worn a lot of hats: retailer, manufacturer, importer, boot-strapper and everything in-between-ers.

I've been awarded puffed-up accolades that could easily make an ego swell. And some years it really did, paired with failures.

I've been called a star entrepreneur, a trail-blazing

retailer and an iconoclastic designer. I've also been called a loser, an idiot, a failure, and an uneducated disgrace.

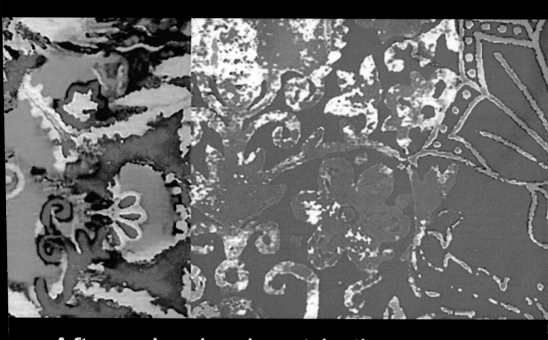

After going bankrupt in the Great Recession, I was shamed and humiliated as we lost so

We had to let go lovely long-time creative employees that helped us build everything by faithfully working their tails off year after year with incredible dedication.

It was a disappointing conclusion following years of growing, failing up, and accomplishing.

I never cried so much, or felt more despair.

Embarrassed didn't begin to describe what we went through. No one was to blame but us. I am more certain than ever that this is true. We should have been better at calculating risk. We should have seen the economic fall coming. But, everything we did proved, time and again, we were bullet-proof. Everyone around us - our bankers, vendors and consultants - businesses that had vested stakes in our success - encouraged us to let it ride.

We bought all that bullshit. Then we ate it. We pushed all of our cards onto the table, and we lost. My god, how we lost.

And honestly, so much more than money. We lost faith and hope and friends - relationships that really mattered.

We lost confidence and belief in our creativity, and in ourselves.

What's truly amazing is that my husband, John, and I didn't lose each other.

You

can't control the

unknown, but you can

take action and inch

something forward

right now.

RIGHT NOW.

Now, on the other side of the calamity, we can identify what went wrong and why. Well, sort of.

I never thought I'd say I was grateful we went through that shit-storm, but I am. We were forced to change everything. We had to dig deep and dissect what we wanted to become next and why.

There have been scores of bumps, bruises and skinned knees, but our ego's are more in check than ever.

Plus, we know bumps are part of the deal. It's how you work through, and learn from them, then push forward that really matters.

We learned that recreating oneself might be as essential as air. We live by it.

If you are willing to be a possibilitarian and you want to start learning how to make your passion and purpose your bitch, and how to unearth explosive happiness in your everyday, then fasten your seat belt.

Whiplash warning...here we go!

Hey, beautiful soul! Let's begin where it all begins...inside you. No one can take away what's inside you. So take a deep look, because without digging, unearthing and appreciating, change won't happen. Not in a million years.

You have to determine how badly you want to unearth your passion, happiness and purpose; You have to ask 'What is true for me?'

It's what will drive you when things get tough. It's the difference between I *want* to be happy and "*I am going to fucking be happy*!"

This isn't a choice; it's an absolute truth that you must own.

ONE BITE TASK

BE HONEST.
IS BEING
HAPPY
A MAYBE
OR A MUST?
THEN
WRITE DOWN
WHY
IT'S
A MUST.
WHAT ARE
YOUR REASONS?
WHAT ARE
YOUR TRUTHS?

Create a list of things you
can do to get unstuck.

Everyone needs to have
their own get-unstuck
manifesto.

Calli is a part-time school nurse who needs additional income, and wants to explore her passion and purpose. She takes micro-action and decides to stop spending money and time each afternoon at the coffee shop (you know what, with a Mr. Coffee and $12, you can make about 20 pots of the best coffee you've ever had).

Then, too, she quits her twice a week pricey Pilates class and finds online videos she can do at home, for free.

Photography and wanderlust are her passions.

She has an iPhone as her only tool, so she purchases a handful of photography apps for less than twenty bucks, money saved from not going for coffee.

After much research, she sets herself up on one of the dozens of stock-photo- and Society-6-type websites; she travels around her countryside town and takes photos of animals, landscapes and barns; and, then she sells her images on mugs, iPhone cases, canvases, throw blankets, and whatever else that will accept ink in 256 colors, all easily made by

others on the websites she joined. Now that's leverage.

Then, approaching local wineries and restaurants with photos she snapped at their establishments, Calli creates custom items for them to sell as well. Turning content into cash.

Her obstacles?
Time, lack of cash, knowledge.

Her action plan?
Excavate time, save money, research options for selling, learn how to use apps.

Micro-steps every day.

Unearthing your passion

Your passion and purpose is, more than likely, right in front of you. It's the thing that makes you to feel like a kid in a candy store when you're doing it. It's something you are likely skilled at, or working hard to become accomplished at.

Did you see that? I ended a sentence with a preposition I was raised that you're not supposed to do that. I broke that rule You're also not supposed to monologue in the middle of an important point but, as you can see, I didn't follow that rule either!

It is where your skill and creativity flourish.

There are clues all around you. It may be the thing you want to do in your free time or the thing your excel at in your job.

You don't have to narrow it down to one thing, many passions are tiered, which is great and offers more opportunity.

If you want your passion to become you're career, be vigilant and choose something that has market viability. Do some research. Read up on it. Find out more.

Otherwise keep it as a hobby until your skill and expertise allow you to transition it to more.

ONE BITE TASK~

IF YOU COULD DROP EVERYTHING
RIGHT NOW AND DO SOMETHING
THAT MAKES YOUR HEART SOAR
WHAT WOULD IT BE? LOOK HIGH
AND LOW, LOOK DEEP INSIDE
YOURSELF AND THEN, THINK
ABOUT HOW YOU SPEND YOUR
TIME...OR HOW YOU WOULD
PREFER TO SPEND IT.
BIG CLUE ALERT!
BE REFLECTIVE.

Beginning is the hardest part...

Firsts are wonderful and vulnerable and mind blowing. It's when ideas fly and dreams should be explored.

You've laid claim to an idea. Now what? In a word [*or rather in a hyphenated word*]: **Micro-action**.

Does the word 'action' paralyze you? Regardless of your education, financial situation or mental health status, paralysis of forward movement and the inability to embrace change is real. It doesn't discriminate; it doesn't care; it doesn't give two...well, you get the point.

To work around it, **force yourself** to pivot and take one step in the direction you want to move. **ONE STEP!!** It can be anything. But you have to move, or nothing will happen.

And the old adage is true, "Nothing stays the same – you're either moving things forward or things are going backward".

One simple, little step a day will add up. It's my number one piece of advice. TAKE ACTION.

You need to ask yourself in all honesty, 'Am I ready take a small step everyday to find my **happiness?**' And if your answer ain't '**yes**' then please close this book now and use it to level your wobbly table or kill bugs or something – anything – useful. If you're not ready, willing and able to take action – even the most demonstratively incremental measure – forward, then you have to start somewhere else.

When I decided to write my first romance novel, I sat down and wrote one scene. I **didn't overthink.** I didn't plot – I didn't even know how to – but I needed to know if I had it in me to write. I had no idea how many things I was exploring and unearthing. My happiness quotient skyrocketed. Why? Because I was taking micro-action and moving perceptibly forward.

Explosive happiness is awesome and achievable.

Say yes selectively, or you will drown in requests, guilt and exhaustion.

ONE BITE TASK~

ONE STEP. IF YOU'RE MORE OF A DREAMER THAN A DOER THEN THIS IS THE MOST IMPORTANT STEP YOU WILL TAKE. IF YOU DON'T TAKE ACTION NOW THEN ZERO WILL HAPPEN. NO ONE CARES ABOUT HOW BADLY YOU WANT IT. TALKING ABOUT YOUR PASSION IS NOT ACTION. ACT NOW AND BE PURPOSEFUL OR YOUR PASSION WILL DISPERSE INTO THE SKY LIKE SO MUCH DUST, AND DISAPPEAR ALONG WITH MILLIONS OF OTHER DORMANT PASSIONS AND FORGOTTEN DREAMS OF EXPLOSIVE HAPPINESS.

One minute muse

India was recently let go from her job as a bank teller. What next? She spends weeks deliberating and procrastinating.

India is a perfectionist and can only find her calm and focus when she explores her passion, which happens to be pickling organic veggies.

She wants to turn her passion into profit by selling her goods. But the obstacles are endless in her mind. Naturally, most of them are invented by her need to have everything wrapped in a tidy perfect little bow. She cannot stop planning, with her spreadsheets, business plans, financial forecasts, marketing plans, SWOTS and asset assessments. Her background in marketing and finance are quicksand to her ability to take action.

Frustrated, she takes a walk toward the local farm stand with a pad of paper in hand. She doodles rows of beautifully canned fermented veggies while considering all the ways she will add her flair to them. Unique labels. Vintage fabric toppers. Unusual combinations of spices and herbs. She's not short on ideas; she has notebooks full of them. But how does one begin?

She arrives at the farm stand still puzzled about how to set things in motion.

As she enters the crowded shed, she watches as a young girl pops a juicy strawberry in her mouth. That one action gets India's creative juices flying. Then her brain goes into overdrive, one idea begetting another as to how she moves her plan forward.

She decides to approach the farmer and see if there's any interest in a private label line of fancy canned veggies, along with tastings on Saturdays at the stand.

Nothing will happen if she doesn't take micro-action.

Her obstacles - Overwhelm, procrastination, overthinking.

Her action plan - Start now. India dashes home. Elated, she creates her first collection of goods. She then makes a meeting with the farmer to present her idea. Her back up plan? Sell her goods at the local flea market on the weekends.

YOU HAVE TO BELIEVE
YOU ARE CREATIVE.

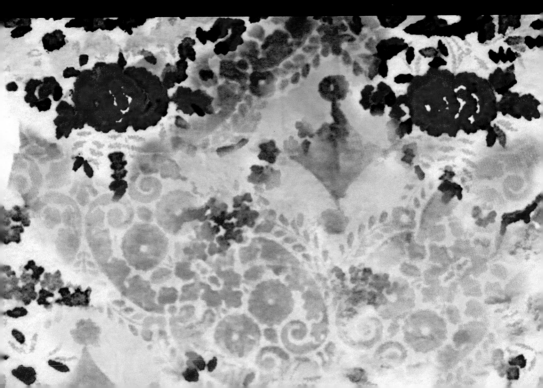

Happiness. You want it. Must have
it. BUT you *can't* seem to explore
your passion and purpose.

Why? Because you're too busy, too
broke...too unhappy. *Cue the music -
isn't that ironic?* You have no good
ideas or zero education. You're too
old or too young. Too unmotivated.
Depressed. Terrified. Insecure. Whoa!
Flatulence?

What am I missing...? Coming up
with all the excuses could take
months. The excuses are endless. I've
been there and I've checked the box
on *almost* every one of those things
I mentioned, along with a bunch
more.

Maybe you aren't desperate enough.
*Sorry. Did that feel as if I
punched you in the throat? Well, if
it did, good. And I'm not sorry.*

I don't want to cause pain - *well,
maybe a little, just to get the blood
moving* - but I can't with good
conscience offer pie-in-the-sky
advice since I've been flat on my
face, ugly crying, freaked out about
my next move more times than I care
to admit.

It's not pretty when you feel that
way.

BUT, desperation can be an awesome driver. Excuses are facades for fear. And what's fear anyway? The idea that you might somehow be humiliated? You can overcome fear, work around fear and make fear your bitch.

Here's a massive clue: The way you get around fear is by taking micro-action. Make the decision to move something - anything - forward. Get off the floor, wipe away the tears, dust yourself off and do one thing. When you do that one thing, what that tells your brain is that it works. No matter how small, action begets more action. The best tool to handle your fear is ACTION. That's your number one weapon.

It takes massive courage and belief in ones-self to move forward. But there isn't a magic pill. There is only action, and micro-action gets action moving
Recognize now that you are desperately hungry to unearth your passion and purpose to find explosive happiness.
Don't break your own heart by being an impossiblitarian. Remember limits are bullshit. Do you want to smell like that?

Don't expect
a unicorn
to make your
life your bitch

Unless you are
the unicorn.

ONE BITE TASK~

DRAW A   LINE   DOWN THE
        CENTER

OF A PIECE OF PAPER.

ON ONE SIDE, WRITE ALL YOUR
BULLSHIT EXCUSES.

        ON THE OTHER SIDE
WRITE AN
           ACTION
THAT OFFERS   POSSIBILITY.

I HAVE DONE THIS   EXERCISE
         MANY TIMES
OVER THE YEARS.

        IDENTIFY,
        EVALUATE,
        TAKE A SMALL
        STEP.

P.S. WHILE YOU'RE AT IT TELL
    FEAR   TO FUCK OFF -
        YOU'RE BUSY!

The Point In Time

Be a time creator. There are minutes and hours waiting for you to claim them, each one a gift of potential explosive happiness.

Can you spare fifteen minutes a day? An hour? Two hours? I'm not saying quit your day job. That's a very big and personal decision.

Make sure you're on solid ground before you do something overly aggressive.

How can you make time? Prioritize. Shut off the TV. Ditch social media for a little while. Get off the internet. Stop talking on the phone. Shorten your chore time. Wake up earlier.

Then, find a quiet space inside or out in nature, and disappear into your own magical action world. You need space to think. Even a tiny morsel of space is enough.

Make time your bitch or it will own you and wolf down your explosive happiness like a starved mongoose (or polar bear...or whatever thing you can imagine that would eat that).

ONE BITE TASK~
EVERYDAY INCREASE THE AMOUNT OF
TIME YOU EXPLORE YOUR PASSION.
STOP WASTING YOUR DELICIOUS DAYS
WITH ENDLESS EXCUSES AND
DISTRACTIONS.

DON'T EVER SAY YOU
DON'T HAVE TIME
AGAIN.

YOU HAVE TIME. STOP SUCKING AT
USING IT TO YOUR ADVANTAGE.
HOW'S THAT FOR SOME WHOOPASS?

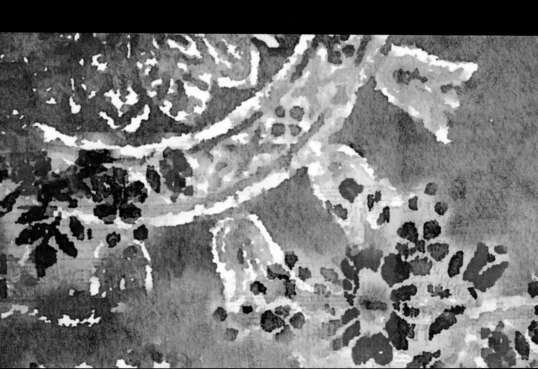

Stella works full time as an administrative assistant. She feels stuck in a rut and unchallenged in her job and life.

She has a passion for styling outfits, so she proposes an idea to few retailers. She'll play stylist for their customers at night or on weekends. Mostly for fun, though in the back of her brain she's thinking it could turn into more.

Two retailers agree to give her idea a spin.

She works diligently to prove her value and shares her style tips and advice for free.

After styling each customer's outfit, she takes photos of them in her creations and then writes about them on her new blog. As months fly by she begins to have a nice following.

She makes a name for herself: *The Hip Aesthetic.*

She sticks to her simple routine and plows ahead. Every day in her free time, Stella takes micro-steps toward turning her passion and purpose into her part-time career. She has focus and experiences explosive happiness!

Her obstacles~~ Stuck in an unsatisfying job, no outlet for her creativity.

Her action plan~~ Micro-steps. Offer her gift of styling as a value to others to prove herself. Turn that action into a potential side stream of income.

EVERY TIME YOU
OVERCOME FEAR YOUR.
BRAIN GROWS

Educate Yourself

Whether you believe it or not, we live in the greatest time ever. You can learn most everything…online…for free! You have zero excuses for not buffing up on your passion and growing your skill set.

I spend the first portion of my day, every single day, educating myself like a ravenous pig. I get a rush when I learn new things. I eat books and blogs and videos and articles and podcasts. I travel through galleries and museums and cities and treasure troves, all from my overstuffed armchair while sipping tea and taking copious amounts of notes. Virtual reality? It's the internet – hop on the DSL train and ride to wherever your heart and mind desire. Open your eyes and mind, learn new things every single day.

ONE BITE TASK~

LEARN SOMETHING NEW ABOUT
YOUR PASSION TODAY FROM AN
EXPERT IN THAT FIELD.
WATCH ONE VIDEO OR READ
SOMETHING THEY'VE WRITTEN OR
CHECK OUT AN INTERVIEW OR
PODCAST THEY WERE PART OF.

WRITE DOWN ONE TAKEAWAY YOU
CAN APPLY *NOW*.

OR TEN IF YOU LIKE LOTS OF
SMALL BITES LIKE ME.

MUNCH,

MUNCH,

MUNCH.

taking action on things I need to move forward if I did.

When I research, I like knowing I can come back to the goodness I unearth.

Pinterest has made my creative life easy to organize. I used to have hundreds of file folders stuffed with tear sheets, along with mountains of books tabbed with sticky notes. I still do

ONE BITE TASK~
IDENTIFY MULTIPLE
WEBSITES, BLOGS, VLOGS,
PODCASTS, AND BOOKS ETC.
THAT YOU WILL GO BACK TO.
MAKE IT EASY AND
INSPIRING. MAKE YOUR
LIBRARY YOUR BITCH AND YOU
WILL NEVER RUN OUT OF
INSPIRATION.

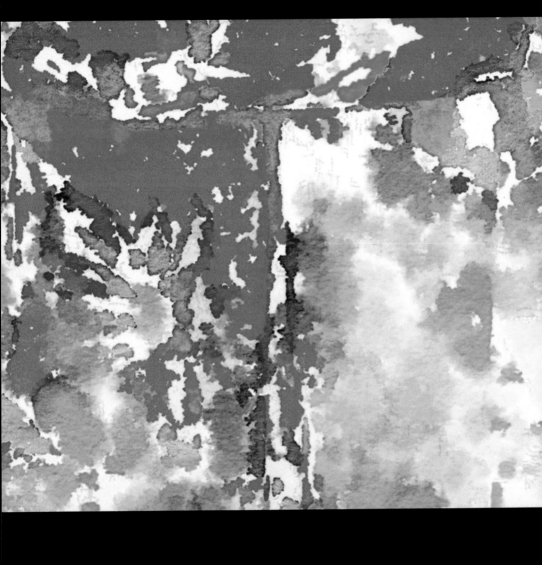

What's the big idea?

Big ideas are fun to come up with – it's like playing. I let my imagination fly when I brainstorm. I allow everything to be a possibility when I'm in big idea mode. I'm certain this keeps my creative muscle lively. How many big ideas do I execute? A handful. And I don't spend more than ten minutes a day doing this.

This series of books was on my big ideas list. I systematically break my list down into small easy to deal with bites. I remind myself multiple times a day; break everything down. It's keeps frustration and overwhelm at bay.

Dream. Identify. Break down. Take micro-action. Repeat.

Move shit forward.

ONE BITE TASK~

GRAB SOME PAPER AND JOT IDEAS
DOWN LIKE YOUR LIFE DEPENDS
ON IT. DON'T OVERTHINK
ANYTHING THAT POPS INTO YOUR
BRAIN. JUST WRITE IT DOWN AND
KEEP THINKING. BIG.

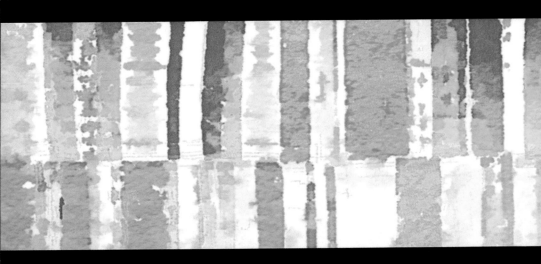

P.S. Happiness leads to
productivity... and so on and so
forth. The circle will keep
revolving. Your happiness will
keep growing. Viciously sweet!

IDENTIFY WHERE PERFECTIONISM MIGHT BE STOPPING YOU FROM MOVING FORWARD, THEN RECTIFY IT WITH A DOABLE PLAN OF ACTION.

I have a simple-as-pie breakdown method. I keep clipboards - stocked with white copy paper - by the dozens always within reach. I also use 3" x 5" index cards nonstop. I kind of have an obsession. Nothing I can't handle though.

To begin, make quadrants on a piece of paper. Write your big idea across the top in **bold**, then write any words, topics, etc. that you associate with it in the quadrants which you can also title to help keep things clear. Don't limit yourself or be intimidated. Idea generating is a skill anyone can become good at in time. Be patient. Practice.

Example. *Make it Your Bitch* book series.

Q.1 Title ideas. Creativity, writing, passion, sex, family, relationships.

Q.2 Topic ideas. Hustle, fear, masks, success, step-the-fuck-up.

Q.3 Key words. Self-help, teaching, art therapy, anxiety.

Q.4 Research. Experts, influencers, creative's, websites.

My brain is on overdrive all day and night. Mental gymnastics make me super happy. When I'm inspired I'm everything I want to be. Explosively happy! Then I take action. You are going to get so sick of that phrase but I promise you, soon you'll be an action hero...as opposed to

a bobble head.

GET SOME PAPER + START
YOUR MENTAL GYMNASTICS.
BREAK ONE OF YOUR BIG
IDEAS DOWN.

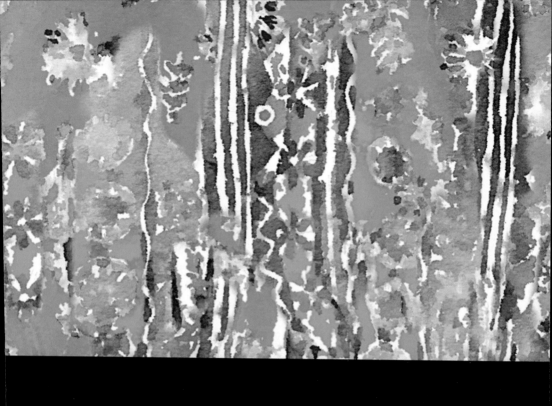

What do you do that you can share with others. Bring value to someone else's life and you will both benefit tremendously.

Axel is a bodybuilder who works
at a gym as a personal trainer. He
subscribes to twenty newsletters
on health and fitness and ten blog
feeds. He wants desperately to call
himself an expert and start his
own vlog.

Distraction and anxiety are his
downfalls.

His inbox is overwhelming and
cluttered, and he gets anxious
every time he scrolls through his
Instagram feed for over an hour
each morning.

He makes a few micro-changes to
his routine by cutting back on
subscriptions and the amount of
time he spends dawdling on social
media.

Then he creates an online library.
Every day he studies, working
hard to become an expert.

His micro-steps give him time to
learn and grow and step back and
breathe. Meanwhile his anxiety
levels plummet, so he begins his
vlog.

Axel is inspired, taking action,
moving his dream forward. By
"doing", he's doing one thousand
percent more than most people
ever will.

His obstacles: Distraction and
anxiety. Life is unnecessarily
cluttered.

His plan of action: Simplify.
Focus. Be in the here and now.

Prioritize.

Persistence…Make it your bitch

Don't give up because you linked a fancy expectation to your passion. Maybe you decided your idea/concept/plan would become X, Y and Z by a particular date but didn't get there. Trust me, I've done that. Expectation causes distress; it does not offer hope.

Don't let a friend or family member tell you to throw in the towel either. If I love a particular thing and it feels like it's part of my DNA (such as, hmmm, let me think… writing and creating), then I remind myself daily. It's my marathon. Persistence matters, though many other people will quit while you're jamming on your passion. Most people want success to be easier than it is. Easy equals painless; painless equals no change; no change equals no happiness.

Don't compare how things are moving forward for you with how they're moving forward for someone else. No one has it all figured out. Keep your blinders on and swim like a mother-fucking Olympian.

ONE BITE

TASK~

WRITE DOWN THE REASONS
YOU ARE AMPED OUT OF
YOUR GOURD TO MOVE YOUR
PASSION FORWARD. THESE
WOULD BE YOUR PURPOSES.
WHEN YOU GET FRUSTRATED
PULL THIS LIST OUT.
DON'T OVERTHINK THIS.

KEEP IT SIMPLE.

One minute muse

Asher is a realtor who went BK in the crash. He loves what he does but he's lost competing in the digital age. It's all too terrifying to figure out where he could fit in.

His competition is *more* outgoing and *more* skilled at networking and *more* tech savvy. They are hungry and willing to go to extremes to capture the attention of buyers and sellers.

So, what does he do? Well, what he doesn't do is nothing, right? Instead, he steps it up. Micro-steps. He decides to rebrand himself as the local guru and real estate expert. And he'll do that making others shine.

He highlights local businesses on his website with photos, videos and inviting descriptions. He creates videos of local residents who gush about the area. He hosts digital open houses that anyone from anywhere can easily access. He offers discounts at local establishments if you list your home with him or buy your new home from him.

Every day one more thing falls into place because of his routine diligence. Who the hell doesn't want to work with Asher?

His obstacles: He see's walls where he could see opportunity.

His action plan: Educate, step outside of his comfort zone, become a local hero by putting other people on the pedestal.

Add Value anywhere you can.

Make reinvention your daily truth.
I thought our first furniture designs,
way back when we were newbie
entrepreneurs, were really cool and
different from anything in the
market. Then we evolved and got re-
inspired all over again. And again.
And again.

Some retailers said we should stop
evolving, because they liked our old
stuff. We stuck with our instincts
and kept navigating creativity and
exploring with passion.

Evolving is imperative to growth,
though you must evaluate your
progress with honesty and humility.

Evaluate why you failed or why you
grew. Take a breath and reflect on
why you are doing what you do.

That's when you'll grow even more.

ONE BITE TASK~

CONSIDER YOUR DAY TO DAY,
AND SPARK ONE REINVENTION
OF YOUR WORK. I DO THIS
DAILY. IT'S BETTER THAN
MEDIATION TO ME.

It's like dessert for my soul

Words and images are free. Mix them up and make them work for you, then surrender to your imagination, and take a step forward.

MATTER TO YOU

Write the book.
Create the art.
Do whatever it is you do because
you want to. Don't do anything in
hopes of congratulatory platitudes.
You'll get crushed when people
don't deliver what you hoped they
would have.

Tiny and realistic expectations of
others can mean massive goodness
for you. Expect that most people
will do zero when it comes to your
needs and wants. Trust me, you'll be
a happier person if you do. It's not
pessimism. Quite the opposite: it's
understanding what to expect – and
what *not* to expect – that will make
you a shining optimist.

Be the best you, and it won't matter
what anyone else is doing or
saying.

ONE BITE TASK~

COME UP WITH FIVE SMALL
THINGS YOU CAN DO TO BE THE
BEST YOU IN REGARDS TO YOUR
PASSION.

(IN ITALIAN)

UNO: _____

DUE: _____

TRE: _____

QUATTRO: _____

CINQUE: _____

EVERYTHING
WE DID
PROVED. TIME
AND AGAIN.
WE WERE
BULLET-
PROOF. WE
BOUGHT THAT
BULLSHIT.
THEN WE ATE
IT.

Most people feel vulnerable a few times a day. It's human. If you're putting yourself out there and exploring your passion. It comes with the territory.

Vulnerability drives our society to showcase our perfect worlds of filtered selfies, ripped abs, award-winning kids, and so forth.

We all know life is not perfect. If you've had a mess of kids, you likely don't have perfect abs. If you're just starting your passion, you are not an expert. If you have a garden, you might have weeds. *Oh, the horror*

I'm in marketing. I share my lifestyle openly and I am not perfect. I'm imperfectly human, or I'm human, which is imperfect. You get the picture.
I'm drawn to authentic people. When I come across a brand or lifestyle expert who is real, I appreciate them even more.

cocktail chats!

When I host Facebook live cocktail chats, inevitably a few people reach out after to let me know that maybe I swear and drink too much.

Really?!

What's a fucking lady to do? The excitement of live video is the rawness, the realness, the rush of emotion. You can't fake authenticity.

Embrace your imperfections as you explore your passion, and then politely offer the grumblers one finger and two words as you delight in your explosive happiness and blissful authenticity.

one bite task

THE NEXT TIME YOU SHARE
YOUR PASSION ON SOCIAL
MEDIA, BE AS REAL AS
REAL GETS. TRUST ME,
PEOPLE WILL LIKE THE
REAL YOU. AND IF THEY
DON'T, WHO THE FUCK
CARES?

RIGHT?

MAKE FRUSTRATION
YOUR FUEL

Some people say they don't believe
in frustration. *Not sure how
someone can't believe in a feeling
but can believe in a boatload of
other crap that sounds really
made up. But that's another book...*

I wish I didn't get frustrated but
I do. I'm on the extreme side of
impatient. I always thought it was
my curse. Now, I own it. I call it
my bitch. I use it as my stepping
stone. And you can, too.

The next time you get impatient,
try my trick. Take a deep breath,
then another five. Then do sixty
jumping jacks or some other
physical thing you can do.
Sometimes I do twenty squats. Or
ten burpees. Or I go outside and
jump on our trampoline for few
minutes. I run hyper, so deep
breaths and movement help calm
me. For some people it's stillness,
meditation. It's something personal

that you've got to identify.

Grab hold of your frustration and work it like you're DaVinci with a lump of cold hard clay.
Reflect and identify how you got frustrated then take an action step. It always comes back to the small steps.

I will admit some inner chanting (yelling) helps me, too. Mine is typically a crazy string of explicative's and personal motivations that create a rant in my head. *"You can do this. You can fucking deal with this. You're better than this bullshit. Stick the landing. Stand up and get back in there. Knock it off. Grrrr. I got this. I got this. I have got this. I fucking own this shit!"*

p.s. don't overthink overthinking.

ONE BITE TASK

Identify something in your current work day that is frustrating you. What small action step are you going to take to use your frustration as a stepping stone? Create a plan you can go back to when you need it the most.

n going to use myself here. Sound
rty? I promise it's not.

got exceedingly frustrated one day
ile back and it got me thinking.
nce I practice using frustration as
 stepping stone – for fear it'll
ush me if I don't – I realized afte
iting down pages worth of ideas th
wasn't doing something very well.
sn't sharing my knowledge.

guess I got hung up – frustrated –
w years back after five big
blishers never even replied to my
ails in regards to a home décor bo
wanted to create. That pissed me
f.
en I discovered self-publishing an
ote a slew of romance novels. Once
ey started taking off, it lit a
nfire under my ass: self-publish
her things; share your knowledge.
ink. Fire lit Engine revved. Focu
t!

swear to you, I was bouncing off

but I'm starting to get better at evaluating the why of it.

As for action, I'm a balls out girl.

Full disclosure: I don't actually have balls or anything else that resembles real live testicles, nor would I – if I had them – ever actually have them out to see or whatever..., but what I do have are varbles, chutzpah, gonads, cajones, nuts, stones, brass clappers, bangers, rocks, huevos, or what else essentially amounts to an all-out zeal for getting done what needs to get done. In short, I wasn't born with them, I grew them! Others might have more talent than me...but I'm in it for the long haul.

TAKE ACTION; GROW SOME!

So, what do you do that you can share with others? What can you do that will bring value to someone else's life and, as a result, benefit both of you tremendously?

For some bizarre reason, people are perfectly chill telling other people – even people they like and respect – they suck.

Everyone sucks at first. Everyone but the finger pointers

The reality is, in the early stages of exploring our passions, we do typically suck. So what? Everyone has to start somewhere. Suck away! But do you know who doesn't suck? The finger pointers. Well, actually, they do suck. Like *Harry Potter* Dementors, they suck the life out of everything and everyone around them. They also never start. Anything. They just tell *you* how much *you* suck. And how great *their thing* will be once they begin. Whenever that might be...whatever that may be.

Work hard to ignore them.

Many people – people who mean well – have bloated egos attached to a bunch of bogus crap. Empathize...it's fear of rejection, plain and simple.

Finger pointers cannot understand how YOU (the untalented, incapable person they are looking down their nose at) are able to do something that *they* were born with copious amounts of talent to do. How could you, you little scrappy, take-action shit?! Just keep moving things forward!

ONE BITE TASK~

REPEAT AFTER ME. THIS IS MY PASSION AND I LOVE IT! I HAVE MY BLINDERS ON; I'M MOVING FORWARD AND IGNORING EVERYONE THAT SAYS ANYTHING TO THE CONTRARY.

CHECK OUT AND GET BUSY

Check out, unplug and log out from
social media.

*What the...? Gasp Oh, god, no.... I
couldn't possibly. I mean, how would
my friends...? Who would...? How...?*
Yes. Try it for two days. Time will
fly by and you'll come up for air
after having an orgasmic
uninterrupted affair with your
passion. The world as you know it...
Will. Still. Be. Spinning. And you
will feel less anxious and more
connected to yourself. It will
center you and give you confidence,
which is something no one gets from
social media. It's been proven by a
silo of scientists, or whatever a
group of them is called, that we are
more anxious from all the time
spent trying to project perfection
in hopes of finding connection via
social media.

- It's like 8th grade all over again -
You're wasting delicious precious
time, time that could be spent
exploring your passion. And in
exchange for what? Likes?
Reactions? Thumbs up? Come on, now
#FOMO - Fear Of Missing Out - is
real. But you'll feel more calm
about things once you walk away and
get busy with your passion and
purpose.
Brains are happier when they are
not over-involved in social media.

Think of the fun you'll have exploring your passion. Forget about the things you're missing. Everyone will be there when you get back from action wonderland more confident and happier than ever. Hell, you might even have something *really important* to share…

HAPPINESS IS ABOUT
SMALL THINGS.

IDEAS AND MICRO
STEPS INCLUDED.

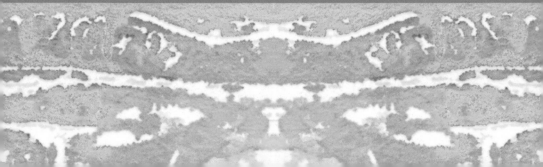

One minute muse

Olive makes cupcakes and finally
found a tiny affordable retail space
with a kitchen to realize her dream
of selling them. One week before she
opens, a well-known caterer down the
street opens a cupcake counter in her
own store. Her concept is identical to
Olive's, which was recently written
up in the local paper.

What now? Throw in the towel? Hell
no! **IT'S TIME TO INNOVATE**

Olive is forced to be creative.
Terrified her dream is floating away,
she jots down every idea she can
muster up. Then she picks one and
breaks it down.

She decides her cupcakes need to be
more than fancy flavors...they need to
be the talk of the town. Out of
desperation and frustration she comes
up with her idea.

She calls it *fifteen seconds of fame*. If you buy one of her cupcakes and read the fortune baked into the middle out loud in a video then post it on your social media – hash-tagging her cupcake store – you'll get a free cupcake the next time you visit her bakery. And these aren't just Duncan Hines smashcakes, they're five-dollar, extremely delicious cupcakes.

Hells yeah, people will do this! Olive not only solved her problem, she is getting great PR by creating a contest for her customers.

Her brain's dopamine levels are skyrocketing! Hello explosive happiness.

Her obstacles – Competition, fear, frustration.

Her action plan – Brainstorm ideas, narrow down, be unique, add value, take action.

Be honest, is this a maybe or a must?

Mondays are marvelous

It's a bummer to me that so many people hate Mondays and cannot wait for Fridays. Try viewing each Monday as a fresh new start, instead of a pseudo-Bataan death march.

```
                        I like Mondays.
They're like second chances.
```

You don't have to wait for a new year, a new notebook or a sign from the Universe or God – or whatever else you're hoping will bestow upon you the power of a second chance. Just take the chance. Anytime! You can start over whenever it works for you. And you can tell the last crappy thought you had to skedaddle.

You can't control the unknown but you can take action and inch something forward right now. Happiness is about small things. Ideas and micro-steps included.

ONE BITE TASK~

THIS VERY SECOND MIGHT
CONTAIN YOUR BEST IDEA
EVER. IF NOT, THE NEXT
SECOND MIGHT...DON'T WAIT
UNTIL TOMORROW. ACT ON
SOMETHING NOW.

One minute muse

Rose is twenty-three and works as waitress since she had to drop out of college due to lack of finances.

She's an introvert and it stops her in her tracks most days. Waitressing was her way to force herself to safely talk to people.

She wants to write novels but has been told by everyone around her that instead she should work on paying down her debt, get a second job and get her head out of the clouds.

After honest reflection, she changes her routine to make sure she can follow her passion and purpose. She wants – she needs – explosive happiness.

She gets out of bed at five a.m. – three hours before work – and takes free online writing classes. Every day she spends three hours educating herself, and every day she takes one small step forward, writing five hundred words...just five hundred words.

And she does this seven days a week.

Sounds tiny, right?But it's massive action, just do the math. 3,500 words a week; 15,000 a month. Rose's first draft on her novel will be done in no time.

Books don't write themselves.

Her Obstacles - Introverted, low on cash and confidence. No time.

Her action plan - Get up earlier. Take advantage of free education online every morning. Start writing every day.

Make a system that screams routine and forward movement, and stick with it.
Is it easy? No.
Is it a must?
No question. Nothing will happen if all you do is dream about it.

THE MAGIC OF
GENERATING MORE IDEAS

I will never forget the first time I was invited to be one of Oprah's guests on her television show. I felt like I was meeting the great and powerful Oz. But, I knew after working with lots of Fortune 500 CEO's, Oprah was not so different from me.

It was just the two of us on set with dozens of my products surrounding us, and my heart trying to escape my ribcage. She asked me, "Do you ever run out of ideas?"

I have the same answer now as I did then. "No."

Every idea begets another. The more ideas you generate, the more ideas will come. It doesn't mean all of them are winners.

The goal though is to be an idea breeder. Make every idea spawn five more. Then make each of those five produce five more each. You have to make yourself do this. It's imperative to your staying power. Most important though is to make sure you don't forget to take action on one or two of them. Without action, notebooks full of ideas simply fill bookshelves.

O
N
E

BITE

O
N
E

A
S
K

TAKE
ONE IDEA YOU
HAVE AND SPIN IT
INTO AS MANY AS
YOU CAN LIKE YOU'RE
A MAD COTTON CANDY
WIZARD AT A CIRCUS.
DON'T OVERTHINK
THIS, JUST SPIT
'EM OUT.

FAIL UP OR FALL DOWN

You might, at some point in your journey of owning your passion and purpose, fall so hard that you will lay face down on the ground and bawl like some snotty-nosed kid who was spanked by Santa and his elves. In fact, I'd put money on it – it will happen. Better to know it's coming and know how to deal with it going into it, right?

So what? Mop up the tears and drool, stand up and take a deep breath. Tell life why you're here and what you're going to do with it.

Own the bitch!

"How?", you may ask....

Begin again. 'Simple' works. Routines and systems work. Don't turn it into a tortuous puzzle.

Go micro. Micro-action IS action. Start from point A, take one bite. Then go to B for another small bite. Before you know it, you'll remember why you found your passion in the first place. Or...you might even find a new one or two.

And don't let any bullshit get in your way, and by that, I mean you. Get out of your own way

At forty-six years-old, and after two decades of being a designer, on a whim I wrote a novel. I know how to take small bites but still, I had a wee bit of fear about diving into the novel pool.

As a workaround, I decided that if it sucked I could always delete it. Safety harness on, I knew I had to try; I owed it to myself to explore.
Then, wow I blew my mind and wrote an entire novel - 80,000 words - in four weeks.

Now that's a cool feeling.

Every time you overcome fear your brain grows. Every single time. It's a scientific fact. Look it up.

Do not underestimate yourself for one second. If you want to try something, even if it's just for fun, then do it. There is no entry fee or red velvet rope with a burly bouncer holding you back. It doesn't require a higher education degree to take a leap of faith in yourself.

ONE BITE TASK~

APPRECIATE THAT YOU ARE ABLE TO GET UP, THAT YOU'RE STARTING AGAIN, THAT YOU ARE EVOLVING.

NOW GET YOUR ASS MOVING. THE WORLD NEEDS MORE AWESOME INDIVIDUALS LIKE YOU, INDIVIDUALS WHO ARE WILLING TO GET BACK ON THE BARMY[1] HORSE AND RIDE THE MOTHERFUCKER UP AND OVER THE NEXT SET OF JUMPS.

[1] It's really a word. British slang for crazy, i.e. *bonkers, daft, nutty, etc....*

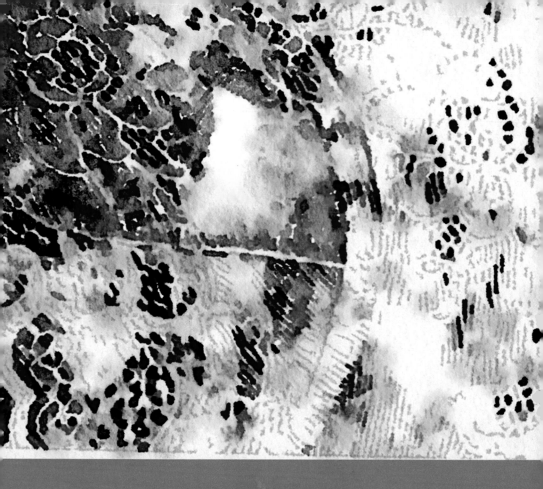

The reality is, in the
early stages of
exploring our passions,
we do typically suck. So
what? Everyone has to
start somewhere.

One minute muse~

Grey's an accountant who's not in love with his nine-to-five. He wants to focus more time on woodworking in his small garage shop where he builds up-cycled doghouses and small funky chicken coops.

He wants to work toward quitting his job or, at least, working part-time.

Another layer: he's a single dad with two teenagers.

And another: he volunteers on three boards and, most nights, comes home exhausted. But he still manages to make dinner, serve it up, do the dishes and all the chores.

Then he spends the rest of his night in front of the TV dog-tired while he nurses a beer, or five.

Here's a thought, Grey ol' pal: PRIORITIZE!!

Dear Grey,

I was thinking of you last night and I thought I'd share some insights I've learned to apply to myself.

1. Quit one or two of those fucking boards. Do you really think they can't survive without you? Well, they can.
2. Make your lazy-ass kids do the chores. They can also learn how to pitch in on dinner, wash the dishes, brush the dog, change the kitty litter and clean those god-awful dirty windows.
3. Unplug the damn TV. You're brain is already turning to mush because you're not solving problems and creating purpose in your life.
4. Lastly, get your ass out of bed one hour earlier in the morning.

Add those hours up and you, my man, just manufactured a lot more time!

With love,

Tracy

Something has to give. Make the hard choices. Make the necessary changes.

His obstacles~ Time management. Excuses. Taking on too much.

His plan of action~ Prioritize, make small changes, pivot and take micro-steps

How To Get Unstuck

Getting stuck stinks. I avoid it like the plague.

Hold up! That's Not even a good simile anymore, "like the plague". The plague that St. Jerome was originally referring to was 1,500 years ago, like in the year 400! Let's instead say, from now on, 'I avoid it like getting stuck'. Sound good?

There are many shades of stuck. More than fifty. Unmotivated, uninspired, unable to see the light, spinning your wheels, to name a few. It often means overthinking and complicating. And it can also mean you lost faith in you and your process.

You have to develop a set of tools to get unstuck, if it happens.

Force yourself to work through the travails and tribulations of whatever has jailed you by jumpstarting your brain. Creativity solves problems in everything: science, business, relationships, teaching...in all of life.

My method always takes me back to a pad of white paper and some down and dirty brainstorming. I'll also spend time online reading inspiring articles or creating new Pinterest boards to inspire me.

Imagery always stirs me. So I have **thought orgies.**

Words and images are mostly free. Mix them up and make them work for you, then surrender to your imagination and take a step forward.

You have to identify what it is for you that rouses and sparks your creativity. Just know there is something out there that will jumpstart you.

You'll find your own special recipe that you can count on time and again. Don't overwhelm with big picture drama. Get your engine started, again. Remember to go micro.

Talk is cheap. Action is everything. I'm not saying you need to be a warrior 24/7 but you need to move. So, take a breath, calm yourself then begin.

ONE BITE TASK~

CREATE A LIST OF THINGS YOU
CAN DO TO GET UNSTUCK.
EVERYONE NEEDS TO HAVE THEIR
OWN GET UNSTUCK MANIFESTO.
HERE ARE SOME PRIMERS:
- READ INSPIRATIONAL QUOTES.
- GO TO A BOOKSTORE AND
  PLANT YOURSELF IN THE ART
  SECTION.
- WRITE DOWN ALL YOUR
  FAVORITE THINGS TO DO IN
  LIFE.
- GO TO PINTEREST.COM AND
  TYPE IN SOMETHING YOU'D
  LIKE TO KNOW MORE ABOUT.
- THAT'S ENOUGH...YOUR TURN.

YOU LITTLE, SCRAPPY,
TAKE-ACTION SHIT...
KEEP MOVING THINGS FORWARD!

Make a system that
screams routine and
forward movement and
stick with it.

Hazel has just graduated from college and now lives with her parents. Her debt load is obscene — she's dead broke and can't find a job anywhere. She's depressed and feeling duped by the system.

She loves yoga — it's her go to when she's overwhelmed with anxiety.

She takes action and decides to get out of her comfort zone by doing Facebook Live sessions twice a day with a friend of hers. Ten minute Yoga for wanna be zensters.

She starts to get a following, then becomes more brave and offers private Facebook Live classes that are more extensive for a small fee. She offers individual classes for a larger fee. Six months pass and she's graduated to ten classes a day, ten minutes each and, holy fuck...she has a cool job.

Now she can take more action and expand on this idea.

Hazel had to start smaller than micro in order to tell fear where to go. For some people small is just getting off the floor. That's okay, too.

Just keep asking yourself, what's true for you?

HER OBSTACLES

Fear. Anxiety. Short on cash. Depressed.

HER ACTION PLAN

Ask a friend to help cushion the fear factor. Start micro with ten minutes.

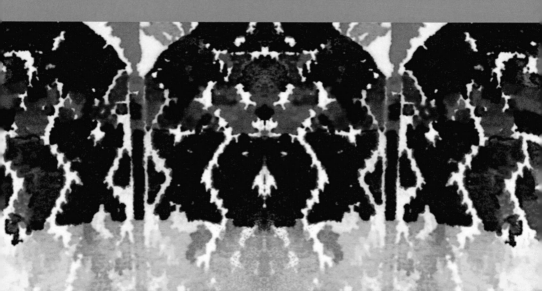

Passion isn't always sexy

We are lead to believe that if we are passionate we will succeed. Oh, and we'll be happy. So is the opposite true as well?

I learned the true meaning of the word passion early on: Bust your ass, while conquering your fears, exploring your creativity and advancing your skills as you navigate the unknown and power through obstacles. Oh, and... fail and fail and fail.

Not too sexy.

Amazingly almost thirty years later this still rings true for me.

It's not as sexy as *follow your passion and explosive happiness is all yours*.

That's because we envision passionate people doing super fun stuff all day every day. Their lives are creative and whimsical and fulfilling. They can talk about their passion like they've found true love.

Okay, sure, maybe some of it's true. But if this "passionate person" is making a living, doing their thing, they have created a *system* and the system includes down-and-dirty hard work and constant evaluation. That or she is one lucky S.O.B.

Some people are. And that's OK.

Discipline. This goes hand in hand with routine, except it's the driver. Routine is the thing we arrive at every day again and again. Discipline is the attack. Discipline means doing the work. The work is not random busyness.

Fun Fact! Checking Facebook every two minutes is not work. It's avoiding work.

Capricious busyness is not progress. Everyone is busy.

Who's really getting shit done? Very few... and, well, now you!

ONE BITE TASK~

CREATE A SYSTEM. IT WON'T BE SEXY, TRUST ME. TRY TO STICK WITH IT. ROUTINE, BORING AS IT MIGHT SEEM, CAN PRODUCE RESULTS IF THE ROUTINE IS FORWARD MOVING, REGULARLY EVALUATED AND STUCK TO.

WORK AT YOUR OWN PACE & IN YOUR OWN WAY

Some people are all about process and rules and long pauses of thought, pondering and tinkering. We all arrive at things differently.

In order for me to do all the things I love, I've learned to trust my gut, to go with my instincts. The end result in my projects is what matters to me. I want to generate work I'm proud of. Creations I look back at and appreciate, even after I've evolved.

Many years ago a creative director at a large company we were licensing with called and lectured me that I had delivered my art *too* quickly. I sent my work to them six weeks before it was due. She told me – in no uncertain terms – that it should have taken a minimum of eight weeks to create what I did.

Then she asked what degrees I held in the arts.

You know what I should have told her: That I've got an MFA in Go-Fuck-Yourself and a PhD in Failing Up.

Instead, I asked if she felt my work was subpar. She said no, that in fact she loved it, and then added she had never seen anything like it. But, she counseled, had I taken longer to create it, it might have turned out *even* better. *Meow.*

I asked if she wanted to send it back, so I could ponder it further.

She agreed it would be the best thing to do.

When my art arrived, I looked it over just to be certain I wasn't being hasty. Then I shoved it back in the box. Six weeks later I sent it back unchanged. And the product moved forward.

If it's good stuff, it's good stuff. Who cares how you get there or how long it took you.

Some movies are made in six weeks. Some in three years.

I really don't understand the fuss, and I'm not going to ponder that thought any further.

Next!

ONE BITE TASK~

EXPLORE A NEW WAY TO
APPROACH YOUR WORK.
CONSIDER TECHNOLOGY IN
YOUR THOUGHT PROCESS.

DON'T
LET ANY
BULLSHIT GET
IN YOUR WAY
(BY THAT, I
MEAN YOU- GET
OUT OF YOUR
OWN WAY)!

your inner critic

Many self-help books ~~advise~~ us to silence
our inner critic. I take that, and most
advice, with a grain of salt. I rather like
my inner critic. She's tough but fair, and
exceedingly lovely. ~~So~~ STUPID!
It's okay to wonder if what you're doing is
good enough. GOD!
If we prance around in non-stop-praise-
ourselves mode, how can we expect to grow? THEY WHAT?
My inner critic is a pretty damn good judge
of my work. I balance it with my inner
cheerleader. Sometimes they mud wrestle if
I listen too much to one side or the other.
I like being humble but I do have to
remind myself I'm doing alright most days.
And, that I have a super long way to go.
This is exciting to me, since growing WTF?!
thrills me.
There is nothing wrong with knowing you
have more to ~~learn.~~ In fact, it's something
to ~~celebrate.~~ APPRECIATE.
Praise, praise, praise isn't a great path to
anything but a bloated ego and likely an
unhappy day-to-day. BLAH!

PICK SOMETHING ELSE

ONE BITE TASK

FORWARD MOVEMENT
REQUIRES RISK AND
ASSESSMENT. WHAT ARE
YOU CONSIDERING RIGHT
NOW THAT COULD USE MORE
BALANCING OUT FROM YOUR
INNER CRITIC OR INNER
CHEERLEADER?

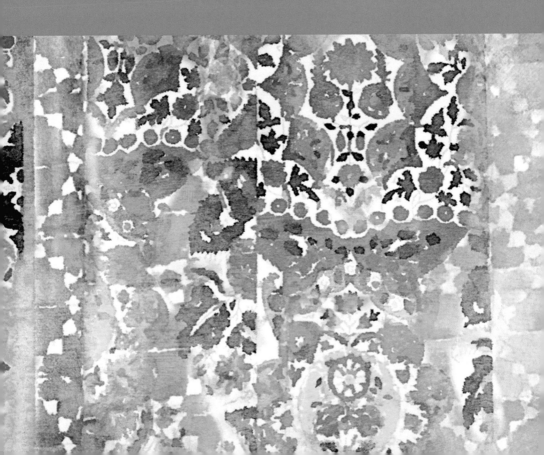

It takes massive
courage and belief in
ones-self to move
forward. But there
isn't a magic pill.
There is only action.

BLUEPRINTS &
OTHER REALITIES

The reality is everyone's blueprint for finding passion and purpose and explosive happiness will be different. Just like your blueprints for love or raising kids or marriage are all very personalized.

I receive many requests for exact recipes for success. If I were that smart and capable I would own an island by now.

This book is not a puff piece. I went into this project with the mindset that I would not fill your head with flimflam.

You can find passion, purpose and happiness when you have the mindset that you are willing to push through stumbling blocks. This takes guts, integrity and doggedness.

I can say with certainty that if you are living your passion day to day, you will go through hardships and heartache. You will also have moments of pure bliss. You will feel skillful and fulfilled that you plotted a course through twists and turns and rocky terrain.

ONE BITE TASK~

MAKE YOUR OWN BLUEPRINT. KEEP IT SIMPLE. NO FANCY DIAGRAMS. NO REPORTS, NO FIVE-YEAR PLANS, NO LAME-ASS GOALS OR OTHER WASTES OF TIME. WRITE DOWN A HANDFUL OF STEPS YOU WILL NOT OVERTHINK.

UNLEARN AND REBUILD.

ONE MINUTE MUSE

Flora recently graduated with a masters degree in communication and PR. She wants to be an entrepreneur. But how, in the overcrowded real world of PR, will people take her seriously since she has zero experience?

Her ideas though...the girl is pure gold! She makes a plan to study the experts like a sniper then does anything she can to help them out. She attends conferences where they speak and takes copious notes on their speeches then distributes them online.

She reposts their videos, their quotes and all their fabulousness. They are the influencers of marketing.
She keeps this routine going every day all the while working a side job to pay her bills. She also aggressively seeks out opportunities with small but hip business owners and offers free advice in return for testimonials of her work.

Flora is all about action, and making herself matter in a cluttered noisy world. Her passion has purpose. She's scrappy and willing to do more than simply show up and assume her degree is enough.

Her obstacles ~ Lack of experience.

Her plan of action ~ Add value. Share what exists. Be willing to do more. Take steps.

the illusion of perfectshunism

AT SOME POINT WE ALL FEEL
THE NEED TO BE PERFECT.

WHAT WILL *THEY* THINK WHEN
THEY FIND OUT I'M NOT?

PERFECTIONISM IS NOT
TRUTH. MANY YEARS AGO I
WROTE A BOOK ON
ENTERTAINING. I REMEMBER,
AFTER IT WAS PUBLISHED, I
FELT OBLIGATED TO MAKE
EVERY ENTERTAINING MOMENT
OVER THE TOP. SILLY GIRL.

I WAS TOO IMMATURE TO
REALIZE NO ONE CARED IF MY
TABLE SETTINGS LOOKED LIKE
THE ONES IN MY BOOK. I WAS
ANXIOUS, THINKING I NEEDED
TO LIVE UP TO MY
BEAUTIFULLY STYLED PHOTO
SHOOTS. WHO DID I THINK
WAS JUDGING?

WHO CARES?

HOW DID I OVERCOME THIS?
ONE PART MATURITY, ONE PART
LETTING GO. MY PROGRESS
COULD ALSO BE LINKED TO THE
FACT THAT WE GAVE BIRTH TO
TWINS NOT LONG AFTER THAT
BOOK CAME OUT. HOLY ROCK
YOUR WORLD.

INFERTILITY. THEN TWINS?
WHAT AN IMMENSE DOSE OF
HUMILITY AND INSPIRATION TO
LET THINGS GO.

I MIGHT SAY MY HAND WAS
FORCED BY NATURE.

DUMB LUCK.

I DIDN'T HAVE TIME TO
CONSIDER 'PERFECT'. I WAS
TOO BUSY TO OVERTHINK
ANYTHING. TWO CRYING BABIES
IN MY ARMS AT FOUR IN THE
MORNING, ESPECIALLY WHEN MY
MILK WOULDN'T FLOW, WAS MY
TRUTH.

IT'S FUNNY HOW WELL LIVING
IN THE MOMENT WORKS AND
FORCES YOUR HAND.

YOU KNOW THE ROUTINE BY
NOW. REPEAT IT.

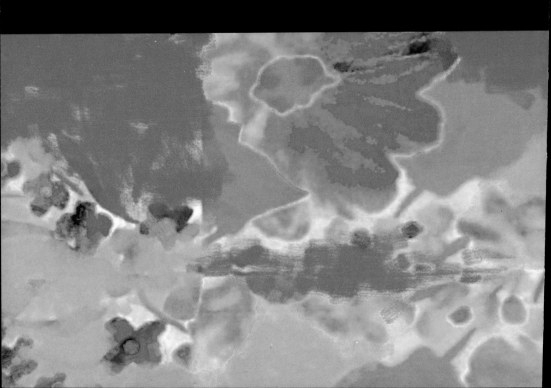

Remember limits
are bullshit.

Do you want to
smell like that?

EGO and expectations

When I published my first book eons ago, I couldn't wait to hand-deliver a copy to my parents. I walked in their front door handed the book to my mom. She turned and set it down behind her and hugged me. She said, "This is wonderful! Congratulations. I look forward to reading it sometime this week."

She didn't even open it.

I was crushed, especially since I dedicated part of it to them.

But fuck if her response wasn't a perfect dose of reality. I wanted her gold medal of approval. Obviously, I had a swollen ego after getting a publishing contract and writing a book. One book. Big fucking deal.

I drove home that night with oceans full of clarity. I had expected and wanted praise. I wanted to be told certain things. I had expectations, none of which were met.

It was brilliant on her part. It made me a better person. I realized that night, how immature my thought process was and how my ego and expectations were only bringing me down.

That's the complete opposite of explosive happiness.

ONE BITE TASK~

WHAT STORY ARE YOU TELLING YOURSELF? ARE YOU DOING GOOD AND PASSIONATE WORK, FILLED WITH PURPOSE TO PLEASE YOURSELF AND BRING VALUE TO OTHERS? OR ARE YOU DOING IT IN HOPES THAT YOU'LL BE GIVEN A SPECIAL MEDAL OF PRAISE, AN AWARD, OR STARDOM?

WHY DO YOU NEED THAT FROM SOMEONE ELSE?

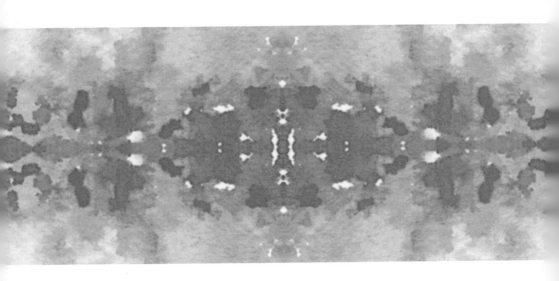

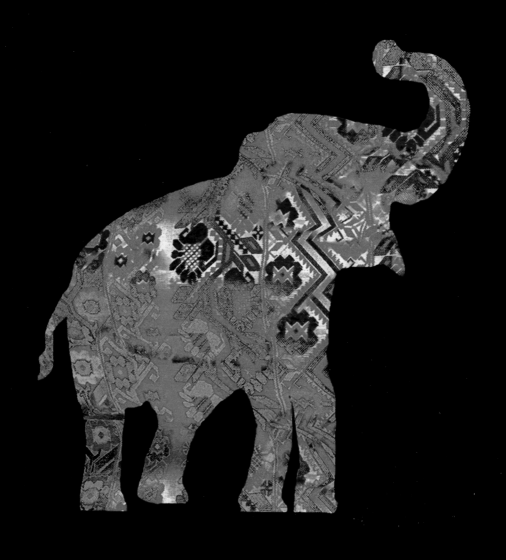

It's funny how well living in
the moment works and forces
your hand.

One minute muse~

Huck is an animal lover and rescuer who has two senior horses that need daily exercise.

He has a goal to help disabled kids since his younger brother is disabled. Trying to find ways to inspire him is something that makes Huck happy. He's been kicking this general idea around for a little over two years. He wants to add value to his community while giving purpose to his passions. But how? And could it possibly provide a revenue stream?

When Huck's brother is visiting his ranch one day, he complains that he'll never have the chance to ride a horse in his condition.

Or could he?

After coming up with an idea to reinvent some of his saddles, Huck decides to offer riding classes to disabled kids. The bonus is that his horses stay healthy while the kids explore something they might never have been able to do.

Is it an income stream or a hobby? That all depends on what Huck wants to put into it. Explosive happiness doesn't always have to have purse strings attached. Sometimes the value your offering to others is the prize.

His obstacles~ Procrastination. overthinking.

His action plan~ Make a move today, stop pondering.

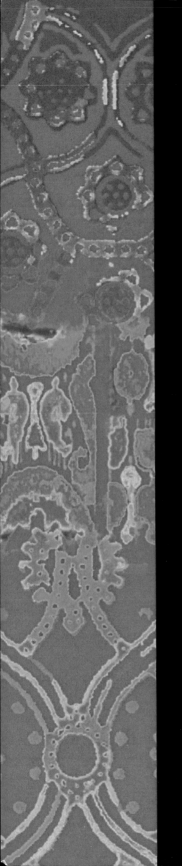

EXPECTATION CAUSES DISTRESS, IT DOES NOT OFFER HOPE.

MAKE REINVENTION YOUR DAILY TRUTH.

SAYING NO!

The current trend is to say
to say 'yes' to everything.
Really? Yes? I'm calling
bullshit, because I tried that
for years on end and I felt
like a pimp to happiness and
my soul.

I will die an early unhappy
death if I say yes to
everything.

Say yes selectively, or you
will drown in requests, guilt
and exhaustion.

I can't afford to say yes to
everything. Spiritually,
monetarily, physically and
all kinds of other -ly's.

Saying yes with a modicum of skepticism might be a more realistic sell. More honest and rational.

When we started saying no in our business to things that felt like flattery, so many wonderful changes occurred.

Pick and choose *yes* wisely.

O
N
BITE
A
S
K

BE REALISTIC. THE NEXT TIME SOMEONE ASKS YOU FOR SOMETHING. EVALUATE YOUR PRIORITIES BEFORE ANSWERING YES. IT'S AS SIMPLE AS THAT. ONCE YOU SAY YES, IT'S TOUGH TO GO BACK IN AND SAY NO.

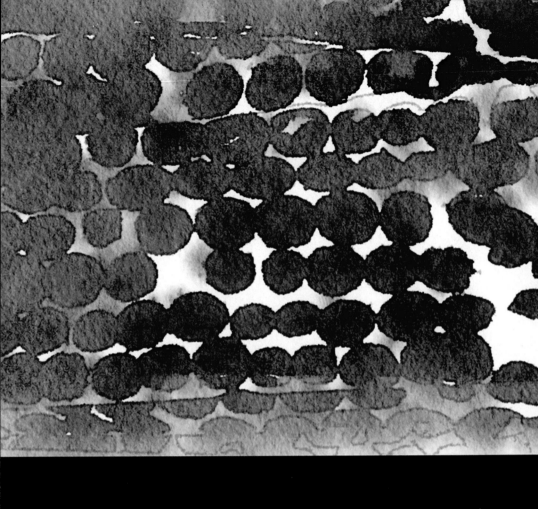

Identify. Determine what's working and making you explosively happy, and what's not. What is true for you. Slow down and really think about this

TRAIN YOURSELF TO
THINK IN
POSSIBILITIES.
OPTIMISM MARRIED WITH
ACTION IS TRUE
DOPAMINE FOR YOUR
SOUL. REINVENTION IS
EVERYTHING.

magic voodoo doo-doo

I've never believed one is naturally blessed with magical wells of creativity.

Creativity takes work. Mining. Self-awareness. Constant obstacle jumping. It isn't bestowed upon a privileged few. It is a skill that can be cultivated by anyone.

First, you have to believe you are creative and can be more creative.

You have to force yourself to explore creativity in new ways. Obstacles provide a great opportunity to discover new imaginative ideas.

Go outside of your norm. If you only paint, try to write. If you only dance, try to doodle. If you only teach, try to make. If you manage, try to garden. Your brain will thank you with explosive happiness.

Train yourself to think in possibilities. Optimism married with action is true dopamine for your soul. Reinvention is everything.

Don't expect a unicorn to make your life your bitch. Well, unless of course, you are a unicorn. Then be a unicorn all the time and never worry again.

One bite task~

This week explore another creative outlet. It can be anything as long as it's fun and something that is forcing you to think differently.

BE YOUR OWN COACH

Though they are trendy and it would be fun to have one, the cost of having a life coach is prohibitive for most of us. That doesn't mean you can't apply life coaching concepts to your day-to-day. I don't have a personal trainer either, but I find all kinds of ways to motivate myself physically. It's again the small bites and action concept.

How to be your own coach?

Identify. Determine what's working and making you explosively happy, and what's not...what is true for you. Slow down and really think about this.

Tweak. Make micro-changes, pivot and advance toward the things you want.

Ditch. Get rid of things and people that make you unhappy. I realize it's not that simple. Some things that make us unhappy

cannot be *ditched* at the snap of
our fingers. In fact, many
things. However, unhealthy
relationships, bad habits and
other downers you are able to
recognize and move away from
are great places to begin. You
don't need to move the mountain.

Cultivate. Nurture and grow
healthy relationships, creative
ideas, good thoughts.

Work around. Find ways to
circumvent obstacles and fears.

Be the light. You are everything
in this process. Be your own
light. Remind yourself with a
constant I-can-do-this attitude
that you can. Happiness leads to
productivity.

Evaluate. This goes hand in hand
with identify. Reflect on what is
working and what isn't.

Take the next bite. Progress is
crucial. Move forward.

creativity

solves

problems

ONE BITE TASK~

A JOURNAL IS GREAT
COMPANION FOR SELF-
COACHING. GET ONE AND TAB
IT WITH YOUR OWN IDEAS,
MAYBE SOME OF MINE OR
SOMEONE ELSE'S. OR A MIX OF
ALL.

One minute muse

Holiday is a quirky twenty-two-year-old who likes making things and has a penchant for finding vintage jewelry on the cheap. She also has a massive love for hand-lettering.

She works full-time as a receptionist at the local veterinarian's office but wants to explore her creative side more.

The problem is time. She has none and her life as it stands feels out of whack.

She decides to crochet fashion accessories then embellish them with her vintage finds as unique gifts for a friend's wedding party. All her friends encourage her to sell them.

Could she sell them? In her mind, she's just a crafter... not a real fashion designer.

She toys with the idea by making samples. Twelve items. Then she hand-letters tags and gives each piece a unique name along with a two-sentence story. With the help of a friend she opens an Etsy shop and peddles her artful wares. A few months in and after a little taste of success she offers customization.

And she adds a collection of crochet dog accessories that she displays in a small corner of the vet clinic.

HER OBSTACLES
Fear. Lack time. Self belief.

HER ACTION PLAN
Work at night. Say no to obligations from time to time. Prioritize. Believe. Take a small step. Twelve items sounds like nothing, but it's a start.

BE A HACKER

Learn to develop workarounds.

I design in all kinds of ways. You name it and I've likely tried it. When I reinvented myself for the umpteenth time a few years back, I had a list of specific things in mind for my day-to-day. I asked the most important question first: what is true for me?

I wanted ultimate mobility to design anywhere, anytime - 24/7. And a space in my home to work as well.

I also wanted the skill to create my designs without others in my space. For years we had a large and gifted team of artists and graphic designers who worked for us. I don't know how to use Photoshop or any of those types of graphic programs. I don't want to. And, I didn't want to purchase unnecessary pricey software with big learning curves.

I wanted intuitive applications that would push me and allow me to accomplish my creative goals.

Sounds pretty pie-in-the-sky, doesn't it? Not really. I was desperate and hungry.

So, we turned the space that was our master bedroom into our work studio. And our walk-in closet became our bedroom, our sleeping nook, our love den. And it's the best place to sleep. Ever. Think gypsy caravan – colorful patterned fabric and all.

My iPhone and an iPad became my mobile studio. I invested about $40 in about twenty-five apps of all kinds: Photography, graphic, fonts, etc., and I was set.

Next, I began photographing chunks of my massive artwork archive, stuff from the beginning. After that I created more galleries of garden photos, textures and vintage fabrics.

I add new stuff all the time. Anywhere I go I take photos of flowers, leaves, textures, etc. Then I tweak and recreate and play. It is endless amounts of creativity and fun. I can take one pattern and spin it into twenty…from anywhere, at anytime. I don't even feel like I'm working.

But I work a shit-ton.

Creating is what I do because it brings me explosive happiness.

ONE BITE TASK

COME UP WITH A FEW WAYS YOU CAN BE A HACKER.
WHAT ARE YOU CURRENTLY DOING THAT CAN BE DONE DIFFERENTLY? WHAT IF YOU LOST ALL YOUR TOOLS? WHAT WOULD YOU USE THEN?

UNLEARN AND REBUILD.

PERFECTION IS NOT TRUTH

Maybe you don't believe it yet but just the fact that you are exploring your passion and purpose to find explosive happiness is brilliant! By reading this you are taking micro-action.

Now, wouldn't it be a whole lot easier to float through your day, lazily allowing the river of life and the chaos of the universe to impale you with its negativity and distractions? Of course. As they say, it requires more muscles to smile than to frown.

You have taken a bite from the delicious cake of life.
You've identified that you want to be your own gatekeeper. So say it out loud and proud:

"I am thirsty and hungry and ready and willing to navigate the wild terrain of passion and purpose.
"I am willing to risk the cynics' sage advice, and I am willing to stand up for my imperfect knowledge as I conquer new roads and unchartered waters.
"I am one of very few – I believe in myself on this massively awesome level."

Be proud of yourself. You are the one who's said, I owe it to myself to be passionate and to find purpose.

Thank You for embracing this book in all its in-your-face, let's-get-things-done spirit! You are awesome!

Now Do!

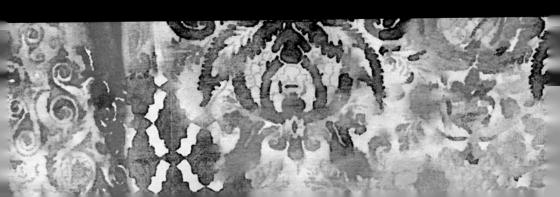

Thanks again for reading this, my first book in the *Make It Your Bitch* series. The other two are available on Amazon: Unleashing Your Creative Warrior and Notes for Creating A Happy Enchanting Soulful Home.

Please take a minute to leave your review on Amazon and/or Goodreads.

For my romance novels, please check out www.awildingwells.com

To see the world of Poetic Wanderlust, www.poeticwanderlust.com

I really apprecitate you taking the time to read this far. Lastly, please take a minute to join our mailing list on PoeticWanderlust.com.

Cheers,

Tracy